Henry and the Great Flood

Gary Richmond

Dallas • London • Sydney • Singapore

VIEW FROM THE ZOO STORIES are based on the real-life adventures of Gary Richmond, a veteran of the Los Angeles Zoo, minister, counselor, and camp nature speaker. Gary has three children and lives in Chino Hills, California, with his wife, Carol.

Printed in the United States of America

012349LB987654321

Library of Congress Cataloging-in-Publication Data

Richmond, Gary, 1944-
    Henry and the great flood / by Gary Richmond ;
    illustrated by Bruce Day.
        p. cm. — (A View from the zoo series)
    Summary: A Christian zookeeper relates an anecdote about a sloth bear's terrible dilemma and draws a parallel with the lesson that we must never despair or stop hoping for God's help.
    ISBN 0-8499-0745-4 : $7.99
    1. Providence and government of God — Juvenile literature. 2. Persistence — Juvenile literature.
[1. Christian life. 2. Bears. 3. Zoos.] I. Day, Bruce, ill.
II. Title. III. Series: Richmond, Gary, 1944- View from the zoo series.
BT135.R52 1990
242'.62 — dc20   90-12333
                                                        CIP
                                                        AC

This book is dedicated to my daughter Wendi, who has learned the benefits of perseverance.

Hi, I'm Gary Richmond, and I'm a zoo keeper. As a zoo keeper, I've learned a lot about God's wonderful animals. At the same time, I've learned a lot about God.

Let me tell you about a grumpy old bear named Henry.

Henry was a sloth bear. Now, sloth bears are small, strange-looking bears. They only weigh about 200 pounds. They are bushy all over, especially around their heads. Sloth bears are mostly black. Sometimes, when they are older, they have a little white or gray around their noses. Sloth bears have funny clumps of hair on the ends of their saggy ears. They are pigeon-toed, and when they walk they rock back and forth.

Henry was a perfect example of a sloth bear. He was as strange as a bear can be. He had several funny habits. If you met Henry once, you would never forget him.

This will give you some idea of how special Henry was. The zoo where I worked owned 16 bears, but only two had names. Ivan was the 950-pound, giant polar bear. Henry was the weird little sloth bear.

Henry often threw angry fits. He didn't even need much of a reason to throw them. Flies buzzing around his head might set him off. Not getting a treat he had begged for might do it. Being let in for dinner two minutes late was a sure way to get him started.

You've probably heard someone say this: "You're acting like a real bear." Well, that statement should have Henry's picture next to it. In fact, I wondered why he was named Henry. Perhaps it was for mean, old King Henry the Eighth of England. I would have named him Grumpy.

As grouchy as Henry was, though, you couldn't help but like the little guy. He was a lot like Snow White's little dwarf named Grumpy. It hurts me to tell you his story.

Henry had a lot of bad days. He liked it that way. But he liked making them bad himself. One dreary January, Henry had the worst day of his whole life.

Around his cave home, Henry had a river of water, called a moat. This moat was built below the level of the zoo's water drains. When it rained hard, water ran into the drains and into Henry's moat. Then water pumps would take the extra water away.

On this rainy, winter day, the ground was completely
soaked. Streams of water were pouring down the hillsides.
The water pumps had been working hard for several days.
And they were getting weak. That night Henry's keeper,
George, left to go home. George smiled at the bear. Henry
was looking through the goodies George had prepared
for him.

Henry didn't even look up when George said good night. It just wasn't his way. Still, this was always the time of day when Henry couldn't hide his joy. He loved food, and he didn't care who knew it. As George closed the door of the bear cave, he heard the happy sounds of Henry eating his favorite foods.

Henry ate and ate until all the food was gone. Then he licked his paws clean. Finally, Henry walked around his cave until he was ready to go to sleep. Soon he was snoring away, dreaming of more food.

Henry didn't know that the water pump had broken. The water in his cave was rising very quickly. At three o'clock in the morning he suddenly woke up. Water was touching his right paw that was hanging off his bed. Henry stood up and saw something he couldn't understand. His cave was filling up with water!

By three-thirty that morning, the water had risen to Henry's belly. Nobody was there to see what happened. But I'm sure Henry threw an angry fit — a real, first-class tizzy! He probably began by jumping up and down on his front feet. Then he probably jumped up and down on all four feet. It didn't do any good, though. The water kept rising and was now up to his neck.

Henry's natural desire to live was now fully awake. He must have walked back and forth; wanting out of his flooding cage. But just minutes later, Henry couldn't walk around any more. He had to stand up on his back legs to get his head out of the rising water. All bears can stand on their back legs. But they don't usually do it for very long; it isn't comfortable for them. Henry wasn't worried about comfort. It was stand or drown. And the water was still rising!

The only light in Henry's cave was a small bulb near the ceiling. It made a scary light that danced across the water to Henry. He looked at the back door. It was now four feet deep in water. Henry wished George would come and make the water go away.

It was now only four-thirty in the morning. It would be nearly four hours until George came to the zoo. Henry didn't have that much time! The water was up to his mouth. He was having to stand on his tiptoes to breathe. He still watched the door for George. And he moaned sadly because he was afraid.

Minutes must have seemed like hours to the frightened little sloth bear. The water had risen even more. Henry was now hopping to keep his head above water. The rain kept coming; it didn't look as if it would stop. Henry's home looked like a small lake.

The zoo security guards knew Henry's moat was filling up with water. But they didn't know his cave was filling up, too. So, they didn't start the emergency plan. They thought the zoo repairmen could fix the plugged drain tomorrow.

George arrived at the zoo the next morning. He frowned at the gray sky and tightly closed his raincoat. The rain was coming down harder than ever. It stung his face and hands as he walked toward his section of the zoo.

When he got near Henry's cave, George saw that the water was waist-deep. His heart began to pound. He yelled, "Henry!" and waded quickly through the icy-cold water. He felt hopeless when he saw the moat around the Henry's cave. The water was deep. He was sure Henry had drowned.

George made his way to the back door of the bear's cave. He reached under the water, opened the door and waded inside. The small light bulb was still working. It shined a dim light in the cave. George's eyes slowly got used to the darkness. Then he saw something strange. Both of Henry's paws were reaching as high as they could reach. Just the tip of Henry's nose was sticking out of the water. George stopped, still and silent. During that silence he could hear Henry's quiet, steady breathing.

George yelled, "Henry, hang on!" Then he ran to find a telephone.

"Security," said George quickly, "call Maintenance. Tell them to bring every water pump they have, fast. Hurry, or Henry the sloth bear will drown. His cave is filled with water. There isn't a moment to spare. Help me!"

Security worked quickly. Soon several men were busy pumping out the water. George was shivering from the cold. But he stood in the icy water to watch his bear. He prayed that Henry would live.

George stared at Henry's nose. Finally he thought maybe there was a little more of it showing. George was freezing, but he would not leave Henry. George had never felt more helpless in his life. He wanted to open Henry's steel door and pull him to safety. But Henry would not have understood what George was doing. He would have attacked George. They would have both drowned before they could reach the back door. Sometimes you can only wait to see what will happen. This was one of those times.

Henry's paws began to slide slowly down the wall. Then, suddenly, his nose went under the water! George's heart began pounding. Had their rescue failed so soon? It had been 10, 14, 20 seconds, and no Henry. George began to wade towards Henry's door. He had to do something! Thirty seconds, and no bear. George fumbled for his keys. Just then, Henry came up out of the water, coughing and sputtering.

In the dim cave, Henry struggled under water to find higher ground. What good luck! He had struggled in the right direction. Henry found the front of the cave where he could stand on his concrete drinker and hold the bars. From there he could last until the pumps drained the water away.

Henry shook the cold water from his face, eyes and ears. He found himself face-to-face with George. George was smiling at him with tears in his eyes.

"Silly old bear," said George. Then he wiped his nose and tried not to cry.

Henry stared at George. His bear brain was trying to decide whether George caused this problem, or was fixing it. He ended up giving George a what-took-you-so-long look. Then he moaned a little to show how uncomfortable he was.

The water in the cave was now draining away. George was sure that Henry would live to throw other fits — perhaps hundreds of them. And so he did. In fact, Henry lived to a happy old age for any bear.

Sometimes it seems as if everything is going all wrong, doesn't it? It might even seem as if you're all alone and no one cares about you. You may feel just as Henry did.

Still, Henry kept looking and hoping for George to come help him. He never gave up! He just kept holding on to keep his nose above water. And that's what you have to do, too, when times are tough. Like George helped Henry, God will help you. Just keep asking him to and never stop hoping.

You see, just like George, God may sometimes seem slow. But he's never too late to save you. Isn't that great news?